DISCIPLINE:
Its Reason and Battle-Value.

GALE & POLDEN'S MILITARY SERIES.

DISCIPLINE:
ITS REASON AND BATTLE-VALUE.

BY

LIEUT. STEWART MURRAY,

1st *Batt. Gordon Highlanders.*

The Naval & Military Press Ltd

Published by

The Naval & Military Press Ltd
Unit 5 Riverside, Brambleside
Bellbrook Industrial Estate
Uckfield, East Sussex
TN22 1QQ England

Tel: +44 (0)1825 749494

www.naval-military-press.com
www.nmarchive.com

In reprinting in facsimile from the original, any imperfections are inevitably reproduced and the quality may fall short of modern type and cartographic standards.

"To secure this, a thorough training is essential, great precision being inculcated in the early stages of the Soldier's instruction, and, later, as much latitude being conceded to subordinate commanders as possible."—*Army Order*, 1*st June*, 1893.

PREFACE.

THIS book is written to try to supply a want which the writer has often felt, and which doubtless many, especially amongst the Non-commissioned Officers and Privates of our Army, have felt also. This want is that of a short and clear account of the foundation—principles, or the reason, of Discipline.

In order that one may carry out any course of action in an intelligent and consistent manner, it is first necessary to get a clear grasp of the principles on which such course of action is founded, otherwise one is always liable, unknowingly, to make mistakes in carrying it out. So it is with Discipline. Unless one has got a clear grasp of the principles on which Discipline rests, of the reasons for its strict regulations, one is apt to sometimes fancy that its restraints are greater than the necessities of order and obedience demand, or, in other words, one cannot see the reason of living at such constant "high pressure," and one is apt to imagine that it is a kindness to the soldier to relax it. From this ignorance of the principles, and consequent inability to grasp the necessity of strict Discipline, there springs an inclination to slur over routine observances, the reasons for which are not understood.

This is perhaps one of the causes of that looseness in the carrying out and enforcing of strict Discipline, which has unfortunately crept into certain portions of our army of late, and which, if it be not checked, threatens to sap the fighting strength of our troops for European warfare.

Discipline is upheld by the authority of the Officers, assisted by the willing and intelligent co-operation of the Non-commissioned Officers and Private Soldiers. It is this latter support which has lately shown signs of becoming weaker; a weakness partly due, as the writer believes, to ignorance of the "wherefore" of Discipline, and a consequent slackness in carrying out what they do not see the reason of.

The chief object of this book, therefore, is to explain clearly *the reason of Discipline*, so that every intelligent Non-commissioned Officer and Private soldier may at once see the necessity of enforcing and upholding its regulations.

The central idea of Discipline has, accordingly, been strongly insisted upon, and constantly repeated, so as to make the manner in which it underlies all the Regulations, as clear as possible.

A further object is to call attention to the fact that Modern Discipline is based upon the principle that a thorough individual training of each soldier is necessary to meet the requirements of Fire Discipline and of future European battle-fields. In Chapter V. an endeavour has been made to show how this need can be met by our Battalion system, according to the spirit of the Infantry Drill, 1893, merely by the carrying out of that system of delegation of responsibility and command to the company leaders, which is there declared to be necessary.

In conclusion I must beg the reader to accept this book in the spirit in which it is written, namely, as a contribution towards the wider recognition and present application of Military truth, and not as an endeavour to promulgate any particular or personal opinion.

STEWART MURRAY, *Lieut.*,

1st Battalion Gordon Highlanders.

February, 1894.

CHAPTER I.

WHAT IS DISCIPLINE ?

Discipline is not, as some appear to think, merely a set of rules and regulations drawn up for the purpose of preserving order amongst the mass of men who constitute an army, rules which therefore need not be too strictly enforced, provided the necessary order be maintained, this is quite a wrong view of the matter, and a most injurious and detrimental one, from which much confusion of ideas has sprung. *The reason of Discipline* lies much deeper. Its object is to implant in the soldier the seeds of victory, by teaching him the habit of instantaneous and instinctive obedience. *Discipline is the long-continued habit by which the very muscles of the soldier instinctively obey the word of command,* so that under whatsoever stress of circumstances, danger, and death, he hears that word of command, even if his mind be too confused and astounded to attend, yet his muscles will obey. Towards this object all the regulations of Discipline, however apparently irrelevant, will be found to tend.

In war the value of this habit is inestimable, all-enduring and all-conquering. History is full of examples of victories gained by Discipline against apparently hopeless odds of circumstances and numbers; so full that to state the fact is to state a truism. Yet it is a truism to which attention cannot be too often called, for, during a long peace, its importance is apt to be somewhat overlooked. Discipline is the foundation of all success in war, and if we wish to emerge victorious from the coming European war, we must tighten up our Discipline.

It may be taken for granted that, with our small army, we shall often have to fight against troops equally well armed, and superior in numbers; to equalize the chances, therefore, we must compensate for this inferiority of numbers by superiority of Discipline. Such being the case, we are the last country in Europe that can afford to permit any loosening of Discipline; on the contrary, as in war a strict Discipline will be more necessary for us than for any other troops (on account of our inferior numbers), so, in peace, our practice and education in Discipline should be stricter and more exacting than in any other army.

This superior Discipline can be best obtained, if every soldier shall thoroughly understand its overwhelming importance, and try to cultivate willingly in himself its necessary qualities, as part of military virtue. Until he does so, he cannot call himself, in the true meaning of the term, "a soldier."

As has been before pointed out, Discipline is the long-continued habit by which the very muscles of the soldier instinctively obey the word of command, so that under whatsoever stress of circumstances, danger, and death, he hears that word of command, even if his mind be too confused and astounded to attend, yet his muscles will obey. This is the great fact to thoroughly grasp, that Discipline is the education of the soldiers' muscles in instantaneous, instinctive, and automatic obedience. His fighting intelligence, and his moral qualities, must of course also be developed, but the first requisite is the attainment of instinctive automatic obedience. This Discipline, this instantaneous, instinctive obedience to the word of command, is what we rely upon to bring us safely through the pell-mell of a modern European battlefield. It is the necessary foundation of Fire Discipline. When, owing to stress of circumstances and of ground, the units of command are mingled in one of those great swarms of mixed skirmishers, which were so characteristic of the breech-loading battles of 1870, and must be equally characteristic of the battles of the coming war; when the soldier has lost or become separated from his accustomed leaders, and is forming part of a new unit under new leaders; when he is astounded by the din and confusion around him; when the noise of rapid fire, resounding from both sides, renders the human voice with difficulty heard; when into this pell-mell rush fresh re-inforcements from behind, and make the mixture worse; when the soldier is too confused to think, and can only act on instinct; at such moments order can only be maintained if *the habit of instinctive obedience to the word of command,* whomsoever it be given by, has been thoroughly ingrained into the blood of every single soldier in the pell-mell.

Let us consider, for a moment, what will happen if this habit of instinctive obedience has not become " part of the being " of every soldier. In the close firefight of the pell-mell his mind will probably often be too confused to think, therefore if his muscles cannot act, through long habit, instinctively for his mind, and obey, no action will be taken on the word of command; fresh units will not be formed out of the mixture of old units, hence the soldier will not know what to do; all direction and control of the fire will be impossible, hence a wild, rolling, rapid, independent fire will spring up all along the line, high, unaimed, inefficient; soon the soldier's last cartridge will be fired away (in the war in Chili, 1891, with magazine rifles, some detachments fired away 180 cartridges in from one-half to three-quarters of an hour); and finally, ammunition beginning to fail, the whole confused undisciplined mass will be repulsed, and shot down as it attempts to retire.

To save the soldier from such a fate, to prevent his forming part of such a confused undisciplined mass, by training him so that his muscles will instinctively obey the word of command, however confused his mind may be,—this is the object of Discipline.

Besides this *habit of instinctive automatic obedience*

to the word of command, obtained only by strict Discipline, *the fighting intelligence* of the soldier is developed by teaching him the theory of minor tactics, and by carefully explaining to him the idea and method of carrying out every manœuvre in which he is engaged; so that (in view of the probable enormous losses amongst officers due to smokeless powder), in the pell-mell of battle, if no leaders are left in his vicinity, he may still, knowing exactly what he has to do, quietly " fight on by himself."

These two cases in battle, when the soldier is fighting in the pell-mell in a new unit and under new leaders, and when, as a last resource, he has to "fight on by himself," are the province of Fire Discipline, and have been elsewhere enlarged upon. We are here only concerned with Discipline, which forms the necessary foundation of instinctive obedience for Fire Discipline.

CHAPTER II.

DISCIPLINE ON THE PARADE GROUND.

Every single individual soldier is an important item in the pell-mell of a modern European battle-field, upon whose conduct at critical moments and the example he sets to his comrades around him, weighty results may depend. Discipline therefore aims at producing in every single individual soldier, without exception, the habit by which his very muscles instinctively obey the word of command.

In considering any question where human nature is concerned, it is necessary first to get a clear grasp of the ideal theory on which its reason is based ; secondly, to make the necessary allowance for human nature ; and thirdly, to lay down the limit beyond which any further deviation from theory becomes detrimental, and which, therefore, must not be over-stepped.

In considering the subject of Discipline on the parade-ground we must accordingly begin by stating the ideal theory thereof, so as to get to the bottom of the matter as much as possible.

Discipline aims at producing in every single individual the habit by which his very muscles instinctively obey the word of command. Instinctive obedience may be defined as the habit by which the brain, on receiving a command through the sensory nerve of hearing, *instantly, without any consideration or opposition,* sends it along the motor nerves to the muscles.

The theoretical bases of instinctive obedience are as follows :

The act of obedience to an order is divided into three periods :

(1) The time taken by the nerve impulse travelling along the sensory nerve of hearing to the brain.

(2) The central period, or time taken by the brain considering the sensation and deciding what to do. (Thought.)

(3) The time taken by the nerve impulse traversing the motor nerves from the brain to the muscles.

Of these (1) and (3) are measurable, while (2) is indefinite. The time taken by (1) and (3) is so small as to be practically of no account, yet to make the theory clear, it is as well to put it down.

Nerve impulse travels along the sensory nerves at the rate of 140 ft. a second, along the motor nerves at the rate of 110 ft. a second.

Now the nerve of hearing is about four inches long,

so it takes an order, travelling at the rate of 140-ft. a
second, only ·0024 of a second to arrive at the brain.
In a man 5-ft. 10-in. high it takes an order, at the
rate of 110-ft. a second, ·054 of a second travelling from
his brain to his feet. Therefore the total time taken
by an order travelling along the sensory and motor
nerves to the muscles is ·0564 of a second, or roughly
$\frac{1}{20}$ of a second.

To this, however, must be added the indefinite
central period. And here comes in the personal equation.
The central period is longer than the other two; even
in the instantaneous process of blinking the eye, it
takes ·0555 of a second. So the utmost possible rapidity
with which an order to march can be carried out by a
man 5-ft. 10-in. high, is:

RE-ACTION PERIOD.
(1) ·0024 of a second.
(2) ·0555 of a second.
(3) ·054 of a second.
Total ·1119 or a little more than $\frac{1}{10}$ of a second.

Foster, in his book on Physiology, states "Roughly
speaking, reaction periods for auditory nerves may be
put at $\frac{1}{6}$ of a second." Also "Practice materially
shortens the re-action period, and *after long practice
the process takes on more of the character of a reflex
(involuntary) act*, with a corresponding shortening of
the interval."

For purposes of this theory, however, it is
sufficient to take the rough average for the three
periods together as $\frac{1}{6}$ of a second; remembering that

by constant practice the central period can be so shortened as to make the act almost *instantaneous and involuntary*.

When the soldier accordingly carries out an order to march or to turn, $\frac{1}{8}$th of a second after hearing the word of command, he is carrying it out with the utmost possible rapidity; until he does so, he has not yet completely acquired the habit of instinctive obedience, as it is manifest that some delay or opposition must be taking place before his brain passes on the order to his muscles. Therefore in order that the muscles may be perfectly trained in the habit of instinctive obedience, no time should be allowed between the word of command and its execution, beyond the $\frac{1}{8}$th of a second required for the order to pass from the soldiers' ear through his brain to his muscles. Such is the ideal theory of instinctive automatic obedience.

As however our material consists of a mass of men differing widely in character and capabilities, we cannot of course expect to obtain this instantaneous complete theoretical obedience. Nevertheless it has been shown by experience that, after making all necessary allowance for the imperfection of our material, we can go very near towards attaining the desired result, if the regulations of Discipline are thoroughly and consistently carried out.

This is the reason that it is laid down in the Infantry Drill that " great precision is to be inculcated;" this is the reason that the greatest possible smartness in the execution of every command is insisted upon by strict Discipline. It is insisted on, not because the motion will look better, as some appear to think, but because the idea which underlies all smartness in the execution of orders is to train the soldier to that habit of instantaneous instinctive obedience, which may prove his salvation in the pell-mell of battle.

Therefore the greatest possible smartness and strictness at drill is most valuable as education in instinctive obedience, and is the best preparation for victory; on the other hand slackness in Discipline and drill does not educate the soldiers' muscles to instinctive obedience, and can accordingly only be a preparation for defeat on a European battle-field.

If the subject be considered from this point of view, the necessity for the greatest possible smartness in the performance of every motion, must be apparent to the intelligence of every non-commissioned officer and private soldier. Those who have thus grasped this necessity should explain it to their less intelligent comrades, so that every single individual soldier, without exception, may thoroughly understand it and try to carry it out on all occasions.

The chief muscles which can be thus trained are those of the legs, feet, and arms, or, in other words, the muscles of marching, turning, and handling the rifle. Therefore, in these three particulars, the greatest possible smartness should be insisted on, as regards every single individual soldier, without exception, always and everywhere. Those soldiers who at first are slow and awkward, should be practised again and again, till, in these three muscular movements, they have attained the same level of excellence as the rest of their comrades.

As an example of how the exact and perfect performance of these motions is an exercise in the habit of instinctive muscular obedience, let us take one of them and consider it in its relation to such exercise. Let us take for example the muscular movement in marching.

There is, as every soldier knows, a great difference between marching at " Attention " and marching " At Ease." The former is intended partly as an exercise in muscular obedience, partly to train the muscles of the soldiers' legs to endure fatigue, and to teach him to take pace of a proper length; while the latter is used when it is desired to get over the ground without fatiguing the marching muscles.

Two different muscular movements are therefore used, according as the soldier is marching at " Attention " or " At Ease." When the soldier is marching at " Attention " he is meant to carry out the muscular movement which he has been previously taught by the " Balance Step." On the word " Quick-March," "the left foot is to be carried smartly to the front, *the knee being straightened as the foot is carried forward*;" it is then to "be placed firmly on the ground, 30 inches distance from heel to heel." This is, undoubtedly, a constrained position, it is not the position in which a man naturally walks—but it is for this very reason that it is an exercise in constant muscular obedience of the legs, and in teaching the muscles to endure fatigue. This is one of the chief reasons that it is ordered in the Infantry Drill. When it is required to march in an easy, unconstrained position, the soldier is allowed to march " At Ease " and to bend his knees.

Therefore, if the constrained attitude of marching at " Attention," keeping the knees straight, as ordered in the " Position in Marching " (Sec. 11) is properly carried out, the muscles of the soldier's leg, besides being developed, are constantly being exercised in instinctive obedience. In marching " At Ease " it is not then the object to train the muscles of the leg to obey the brain, but merely to get over the ground with the least fatigue possible to the marching muscles. This is the great difference between marching at " Attention " and marching " At Ease," and it must be understood and constantly borne in mind by all, otherwise the soldier cannot see why he should be required to march in a constrained position—" both knees to be kept straight " when at " Attention "—and will try to slur over the marching at " Attention," and march in the natural step of " At Ease "; that is to say, he will bend his knees.

Every officer, non-commissioned officer, and private soldier, well knows that this is so; that the balance step is often not properly carried out in the quick march, and that, when marching at " Attention," the soldier is frequently allowed to bend his knees, which is proper only when marching " At Ease." That is to say, on the order " Quick-March, " exact and instantaneous obedience frequently is not insisted on; but by such loose Discipline all the advantages of the carefully thought-out training of the soldier in instinctive muscular obedience are lost. The motion of marching at " Attention " (knee to be straightened as the foot is carried forward), is ordered for a particular purpose, that is to say, it is ordered so as to train the muscles of the soldier's leg in instinctive, unquestioning obedience. If, however, the motion is not carried out exactly as ordered, if the soldier is allowed to bend his knee when the order says that it is to be straightened, then this purpose cannot be achieved, and marching at " Attention " is made valueless as an exercise in unquestioning, automatic obedience. The soldier, in fact, is then allowed to consider how much of the order it is necessary to obey, and to obey only half of it—whereas, the whole object of Discipline is to train him in the habit of exact, unquestioning, instantaneous obedience to any word of command. Such slackness in marching at "Attention," therefore, not only fails to carry out the great object of Discipline, but it works in exactly a contrary direction, by accustoming the soldier to only half obey an order.

A similar analysis of the motions of the muscles of the feet and arms, or in other words, of the motions of turning and of handling the rifle, will convince every non-commissioned officer and private soldier why it is absolutely necessary that the greatest possible exactness and smartness must be insisted on in the performance of these motions, regarded as exercises in instinctive, instantaneous obedience of the muscles to an order received by the brain and thence passed on to the muscles.

Every soldier must further understand that the reason of this strict Discipline on the parade-ground, this instruction in the habit of instantaneous, instinctive obedience to the word of command, is, not merely that the close-order drill may present a smart appearance, but that its object is to carry him victoriously through the utmost stress of modern battle; and that by this means only can he hope to fight successfully in that most difficult position of all, as part of a new unit hastily formed under a strange leader out of that mixture of old units which constitutes the pell-mell of a modern battle-field. In such a pell-mell *his salvation will depend upon his Discipline, upon his habit of instinctive obedience.* That he may emerge victorious from such a desperate struggle, this is the object of his strict close-order drill on the parade-ground.

CHAPTER III.

DISCIPLINE OFF THE PARADE-GROUND.

It is not sufficient that the soldier should be trained to the habit of instantaneous, instinctive obedience merely on the parade-ground. In order that this habit may be properly kept up, *it must never be relaxed*; it is therefore further necessary that its exercise be insisted on always and everywhere, on the parade-ground, in the field, and in quarters.

If it be not thus insisted on, the soldier is somewhat apt to fancy that smart, instantaneous obedience is only required on the parade-ground, whereas the whole object of his close-order drill is to thoroughly imbue him with the habit of instantaneous, instinctive obedience, merely that he may carry it with him into the field.

The soldier must therefore never be permitted for a moment to suppose that there can possibly be two ways of obeying an order. He must thoroughly understand that there is only one possible way, namely :—instantaneous obedience, that if he is at " Attention " all his movements must be as smartly performed when he is off the parade-ground as if he were on it.

Otherwise the habit of instantaneous, instinctive obedience learnt on the parade-ground will be weakened by the habit of slow or partial obedience acquired off the drill-ground; the result being that the great lesson of instinctive obedience, which it is the chief object of Discipline to teach, will not be properly learnt. And what will be the probable fate of a badly-disciplined soldier on a European battle-field, has been already pointed out, namely, disaster and death. Therefore it is necessary that *every soldier, for his own interest,* be trained to instantaneous, instinctive obedience under all circumstances, on the parade-ground and off it.

Every non-commissioned officer, therefore, who, when no officer is by, passes over any slowness or slovenliness in the obeying of his orders, *far from doing the soldier a kindness, does him an injury*; as such looseness of Discipline tends to nullify the beneficial effect of his previous training, and may lead him to the fate of the badly-disciplined on a European field of battle. This truth every non-commissioned officer should thoroughly grasp and ponder over; it may help him in the proper discharge of his duties.

It is now clear that off the parade-ground, when the soldier is at "Attention," it must always be insisted that his movements in marching, in turning, and in handling of arms, shall be as instantaneous and smart as if he were marching past.

In order that this principle may be thoroughly carried out, the very strictest line must be drawn between the soldier when at "Attention" and when "At Ease." At all marching of parties, on the ranges, at all route-marching, at all exercises in the field, when the soldier is at "Attention," the same smartness in the motions of marching (knees to be kept straight,) of turning, and of handling of arms, must always be insisted on as if he were marching past. It is, however, desirable, in order that the marching at "Attention" may not be slurred over through becoming, so to speak, "too hackneyed," that it should not be used too often or for too long a period. Whilst at "Attention" every non-commissioned officer should give his orders in the most decisive, emphatic tone, and insist on the utmost smartness of every motion; but, whenever possible, the soldier should be allowed to march "At Ease."

It is unfortunately a fact that this perfect smartness of all his motions, this parade-marching of the soldier when at "Attention" off the parade-ground has often of late not been sufficiently insisted on, through some mistaken notion of kindness and indulgence to the soldier. It is, however, no kindness, but, on the contrary, an injury to the soldier, for he is thereby allowed to acquire a most harmful habit of slow instead of instantaneous obedience; the habit of only partially carrying out an order.

This habit, if allowed to creep into his mind, works in a contrary direction to, and tends to nullify, the habit of instantaneous, instinctive, automatic obedience, implanted in him by his close-order drill. This fact every non-commissioned officer should bear always in his mind; and he must further remember that one ot his chief duties is to prevent the soldier acquiring this harmful habit of half-obedience to an order, by always insisting on the utmost smartness when at "Attention," as regards every single individual soldier without exception always and everywhere.

As regards Discipline in quarters, if we consider the subject with a view to getting to the bottom of it, we find the same principle underlying its regulations. Here also, if a soldier receives an order, instantaneous obedience must be insisted on by every non-commissioned officer, not merely in order that the thing may be done more quickly, but in order that the soldier may never be allowed to get into the habit of partial or slow obedience; in order to constantly strengthen the habit of instantaneous obedience implanted by his close-order drill, *by never allowing it for a moment to be ignored.*

It is an unfortunate fact that insubordination in quarters has lately become one of the most common military offences. This is due, undoubtedly, to defective Discipline. It is, perhaps, also partly due to ignorance on the part of the soldier as to the "reason" of the restraints and regulations of Discipline; it also points to the fact that his mind and muscles have not been so thoroughly disciplined that the word of command acts like a kind of electric shock, and to the fact that he has been allowed to acquire the habit of slow or half obedience to an order, from whence the step to disobedience is but a short one.

The remedy for this state of things is to train the soldier to such a habit of exact, instantaneous, automatic obedience, that it shall become an instinct, and never to allow the pernicious habit of slow obedience for a moment to get hold of his mind. If the soldier can once thoroughly acquire the habit of instinctive obedience, it will be sufficient to enable him to overcome any inclination or temptation towards insubordination.

Every soldier must also be made to thoroughly understand the magnitude of the offence of insubordination, and the necessity of always checking it in himself and of trying to prevent any comrade giving way to it. He must clearly grasp that insubordination strikes at the root of all Discipline, completely nullifies his training in peace, and utterly unfits him to fight on a European battle-field, where only those soldiers with deeply-rooted instincts of obedience will be of any value.

How can a soldier so badly disciplined that insubordination is possible with him, expect to be anything but a useless, confused member of the pell-mell firing line in the close fire-fight of a European battle-field ? where his mind will often be too astounded to act, and his whole efficiency will depend upon his power, or habit, of instinctive obedience, so that he may be able to obey any order which he can hear, even if fighting as one of a new unit under a strange leader. This power of instinctive obedience can only be acquired by long habit. He must think this out, and he will then understand that any soldier who gives way to insubordination is really implanting in himself the seeds of future uselessness in European battle, and undoing the whole beneficial effect of his previous training.

Insubordination is therefore a dangerous disease, which, on its first appearance in a soldier, must be at once stamped out, or he will become useless for fighting on a European battle-field. No non-commissioned officer must ever pass over any act of disrespect or insubordination, for this reason, that if the seeds of disobedience, thereby shown, are not promptly eradicated from the soldier, they will remain to bear disastrous results on some future field of battle. As these results will probably prove fatal to the soldier, it is necessary *for his own interest*, that the spirit of insubordination be never allowed to remain unchecked in him for a moment.

CHAPTER IV.

DISCIPLINE ON THE BATTLE-FIELD.

If we turn to history we find the same story running through all the centuries; we find the better-disciplined troops ever victorious. The wild, headlong charge of undisciplined valour has, indeed, sometimes swept over disciplined troops and won the day, but such instances are very rare, and have been of no lasting avail against the steady re-advance of Discipline ; always in the long run Discipline has conquered.

In the beginning of history, we find the disciplined troops of Egypt and Assyria conquering all the nations. Later, the Greek Phalanx, and after that the Roman Legion, triumphed over every foe. At Hastings, the better-disciplined Normans were victorious over Saxon valour. After the first rush of enthusiasm in the Crusades had passed away, it was the disciplined, military Orders of the Temple and of St. John who alone upheld the fortunes of the Cross. At Bannockburn, the better-disciplined Scottish Army triumphed over numbers. At Cressy, Poictiers, Agincourt, the better-disciplined English conquered the French; and at Navaretta, the Spaniards. At Granson and Morat, the disciplined Swiss scattered the chivalry of Charles the Bold. At Pavia, the disciplined troops of Spain so shattered the forces of France, that at the close of that desperate fight, in the words of the captive French monarch : " All was lost, except Honour ! "

Perhaps a fiercer struggle has seldom been fought out than that of the great siege of Malta, between the Knights of St. John and the Turks, under the famous Dragut the Corsair. The spirit in which this struggle was fought and won by the Knights of Malta, was that of absolute, unquestioning obedience to their Grand Master, John de la Valette ; the fame of the heroic defenders of the blood-stained ruins of St. Elmo will ever survive as an example of obedience faithful unto death. In the Thirty Years' War, we again find Discipline triumphant under Gustavus Adolphus and the Swedish Army ; the glory of the Yellow Regiment at Lutzen, who, refusing to be driven back again after the second advance across the trenches, fell shoulder to shoulder in their ranks as they stood, is not yet forgotten. During the wars of Frederick the Great, Discipline again asserted its ever-conquering power, and finally emerged victorious from a seven years' struggle against the combined forces of Europe.

In times more nearly approaching to our own, the triumphs of Discipline are so numerous, that it is impossible, in a limited space, to do more than mention a few out of the many instances.

It would perhaps be difficult to select a better example of the value of a thorough training in Discipline during peace previous to action in war, than that of the famous Light Division in the Peninsula. In Napier's " History of the Peninsula War," we find the following illustrative passages : " Meantime Crawfurd commenced a series of remarkable operations. His three regiments of infantry were singularly well-fitted for any difficult service; they had been for several years under Sir John Moore, and being carefully disciplined in the peculiar school of that great man, came to the field with such a knowledge of arms, that in six years of real warfare, no weakness could be detected in their system." " Seven minutes sufficed for the Division to get under arms in the middle of the night ; and a quarter of an hour, night or day, to bring it to the alarm posts, with the baggage loaded and assembled at a convenient distance in the rear. And this not upon a concerted signal, or as a trial, but at all times, and certain."

With these troops upon the Coa, " Braving the whole French Army he had kept, with a weak Division, for three months within two hours' march of 60,000 men, appropriating the resources of the plains entirely to himself." We see that their Discipline was equal to all the emergencies of battle, for in the combat of the Coa, where Crawfurd, with his 4,000 infantry and 1,100 cavalry, braved 24,000 infantry and 5,000 cavalry under

Marshal Massena, during the critical retreat to the bridge, "There was no time to array the line, no time for anything but battle; every captain carried off his company as an independent body, and joining as he could with the 95th or 52nd, the whole presented a mass of skirmishers, acting in small parties and under no regular command; yet each confident in the courage and Discipline of those on his right and left, and all regulating their movements by a common discretion, and keeping together with surprising vigour."

With these troops General Crawfurd made his famous march to the battle-field of Talavera, "And leaving only 17 stragglers behind, in 26 hours they had crossed the field of battle in a close and compact body, having in that time passed over 62 English miles, and in the hottest season of the year, each man carrying from 50 to 60 pounds weight upon his shoulders."

At the critical moment of the battle of Talavera, when it appeared as if the French would succeed in breaking through the centre of the position, Napier thus describes that counter-attack of the 48th which restored the battle. "Hill's and Campbell's Divisions, on the extremities of the line, still held fast: but the centre of the British line was absolutely broken, and the fate of the day seemed to incline in favour of the French, when suddenly, Colonel Donellan with the 48th Regiment, was seen advancing through the midst of the disordered masses. At first it seemed as if this regiment must be carried away by the retiring crowds, but wheeling back by companies, it let them pass through the intervals and then, resuming its proud and beautiful array, marched against the right of the pursuing columns, and plied them with such a destructive musketry, and closed upon them with such a firm and regular pace, that the forward movement of the French was checked."

At the battle of Albuera, Napier's account of the victorious advance, at the decisive moment, of the Fusilier Brigade, 7th and 23rd Regiments, under General Cole, and of Colonel Abercrombie's Brigade of the 2nd Division, is well known.

" Such a gallant line, issuing from the midst of the smoke and rapidly separating itself from the confused and broken multitude, startled the enemy's heavy masses, which were increasing and pressing forward as to an assured victory ; they wavered, hesitated, and then, vomiting forth a storm of fire, hastily endeavoured to enlarge their front, while a fearful discharge of grape from the artillery whistled though the British ranks. Cole and three colonels fell mortally wounded, and the Fusilier Battalions, struck by the iron tempest, reeled and staggered like sinking ships. Suddenly and sternly recovering, they closed on their terrible enemies, and then was seen with what strength and majesty the British soldier fights. In vain did Soult, by voice and gesture, animate his Frenchmen ; in vain did the hardiest veterans, extricating themselves from the crowded columns, sacrifice their lives to gain time for the mass to open out on such a fair field ; in vain did the mass itself bear up, and fiercely striving, fire indiscriminately upon friends and foes, while the horsemen, hovering on the flank, threatened to charge the advancing line. Nothing could stop that astonishing infantry. No sudden burst of undisciplined valour, no nervous enthusiasm, weakened the stability of their order; their flashing eyes were bent upon the dark columns in their front; their measured tread shook the ground, their dreadful volleys swept away the head of every formation; their deafening shouts overpowered the dissonant cries that broke from all parts of the tumultuous crowd, as foot by foot, and with a horrid carnage, it was driven by the incessant vigour of the attack to the furthest verge of the hill. In vain did the French reserves, joining with the struggling multitude, endeavour to sustain the fight; their efforts only increased the irremediable confusion, and the mighty mass, giving way like a loosened cliff, went headlong down the ascent. The rain flowed after in torrents discoloured by blood, and 1,500 unwounded men, the remnant of 6,000 unconquerable British soldiers, stood triumphant on the fatal hill."

At Maya, 2,600 British troops, under General Stewart, re-inforced towards the end of the fight, by another 1,000 men, successfully resisted the attack of 11,000 French veterans under Count D'Erlon. Here, for nearly half-an-hour, 400 of the Gordon Highlanders kept 3,000 Frenchmen at bay, and stretched 1,000 of them on the field. In the "military memoirs" of an officer of this regiment who was present, we read, " At this period the space between the combatants was not more than 120 paces, while the numerical force of the enemy was nearly eight to one against us." " The 92nd directed the whole of their fire against that part of the French force stationed on the brow of the ravine nearest themselves, and which was *so coolly and admirably given*, that in ten minutes the enemy's dead lay literally in heaps. The slaughter was so appalling indeed, that the utmost efforts of the French officers to make their men advance in front of their slain, failed." " For more than twenty minutes the Highlanders sustained the unequal conflict, at the expiry of which, more than half of their men had been killed or wounded, and all the officers wounded and borne from the field, but two lieutenants." Well might Count D'Erlon afterwards remark, on learning that there had been only 400 Highlanders in front of his 3,000 Frenchmen, " Well, then, Colonel, they were not men they were devils,—for before that body of troops I lost one thousand killed and wounded." Napier, in his history of the war, pays no more than a just tribute to their unflinching gallantry, when he observes " The stern valour of the 92nd would have graced Thermopylæ."

Such were the triumphs won by British Discipline in the past, against the proudest soldiers and the most skilful commanders of Europe. If, in the coming war, we would emulate those triumphs, we must first emulate that Discipline. Those triumphs were won by troops trained in a strict Discipline perfectly suited to the battle-conditions of the past; we must look to it that our Discipline be as strict, and as perfectly suited to the battle-conditions of the present. Soon we shall stand once more arrayed in battle against European troops; whether the victories of the past will then be repeated, or not, will depend to a great extent upon whether our Discipline fulfils the above condition, or not.

We require, as of old, a perfect Discipline to carry us forward through the fire whilst the units of command can still be kept distinct, and, in addition, a perfect Fire Discipline, thoroughly engrained into the blood of every individual soldier, to enable us to still fight on in "order," when, by the dissolving effect of the breech-loader and the long-continued stress of modern battle, the original units have become mixed in the pell-mell firing line.

Only if we thus carefully recognise and prepare for the requirements of the present, can we hope to emulate the glories of the past.

In the great Franco-German War of 1870, where for the first time, breech-loader fought against breech-loader, we find the same story of superior Discipline underlying all the triumphs of the Germans. True it is, that on the general theatre of war, they possessed an overwhelming superiority of numbers, and that these superior numbers were used with the greatest skill to achieve the most decisive results; but, yet, at the actual points of conflict, they were often for long in inferior numerical strength to their adversaries, still they were ever victorious. What was it which enabled the German troops, with inferior numbers, to bear up successfully through the long hours of Wœrth, Spicheren, Colombey-Nouilly, Vionville-Mars-la-Tour, till the anxiously-expected reinforcements arrived to turn those fierce struggles into victories? What was it but superior Discipline, but obedience to the word of command become by habit instinctive? Let those who fought in that great war speak for themselves.

In the "Letters on Infantry," of Prince Kraft zu Hohenlohe-Ingelfingen, we find the following passage:

"Each soldier takes it for granted that any such orders will be the best possible. No one ever heard any argument about this, or any fault-finding. Such orders as came were accepted simply as fate. 'Such is the order,' was ever a magic word in our Army, and even though half the men fell in carrying it out, yet the other half executed it to the utmost. This spirit enabled our Headquarter Staff to move the troops as if they were chessmen. It has never happened with us, though often with other armies, that the troops have failed to reach the point to which they have been ordered to march. It was ordered, therefore it was done."

In the "Tactical Deductions," of V. Bogoslawski, he thus speaks of the Discipline which he saw.

"The German Infantry moved under artillery fire often in double column of half-companies; they bore the artillery fire remarkably well. The cases were rare, indeed, when the advance of our infantry was sensibly checked by artillery fire. The French bore it very badly, *as perfect Discipline is necessary to enable troops to stand this test.* When a shell burst in the midst of a German battalion it closed its ranks again, and every soldier advanced, *instinctively obeying* the voice of his leader; but a French battalion, in the same case, would break up, and it took some time to get it together again."

And again we find:

"By the time the skirmishers approached, the French had already brought up their supports, who, however, dispersed much more than out supports did, *as they had not sufficient Discipline.*" He emphatically declares, after having "struggled for days in the bloody mêlée," that "*to carry on a large skirmishing action the very strictest Discipline is necessary.*"

It is instructive to notice the effect of artillery on inferior disciplined troops; for, in the coming war, the man-killing power of artillery will be still greater than in 1870, and will therefore require a still stricter Discipline to withstand it. In the " Letters on Artillery," of Prince Kraft zu Hohenlohe-Ingelfingen, we read how when the Artillery of the Guard Corps arrived on the crest of the St. Privat-Amanvilliers Ridge, "The enemy's skirmishers were flying before ours. But about 500 paces in front masses of infantry were advancing in quarter-column to drive our skirmishers back. You can scarcely imagine the effect which the first shot of

Pritwitz produced on these masses. In an instant they became motionless as if they had received a violent electric shock. But when shell after shell began to burst in their midst, and when my other batteries arrived in turn at a galop, the column broke and fled." "Shortly after we saw the French issue from the direction of Amanvilliers towards us in quarter-column for a counter-attack. We first saw them as they came over the brow of the hill at 1,900 yards; my guns opened a rapid fire, and soon the French were enveloped in the smoke of bursting shells. Then we saw the red trousers as they emerged from the smoke. I stopped the fire. A trial shot was fired at 1,700 yards range, and when the advancing infantry reached that point, I again opened rapid fire. We did this at 1,500, 1,300, 1,100 and 900 yards, when at last they broke and fled. Two regiments (6 battalions) had been sent on this duty." "These infantry attacks were repeated twice more, but not with the same energy; we stopped them at about 1,500 yards."

On the other hand, as an example of what Discipline can do, may be instanced the advance of the Fusiliers of the 74th Regiment at Spicheren, from the Ehrenthal to the Rotherberg, across 1,500 yards of open ground under a heavy artillery and infantry fire, without breaking their ranks or returning a shot.

At St. Quentin the 3rd Battalion, 33rd East Prussian Fusiliers was standing deployed for attack, but had not yet begun to advance, when the main body which stood in half-battalion column was suddenly struck by artillery fire, several casualties taking place. The officer commanding the battalion at once loudly gave the order, "Attention," "Slope Arms," "Right Turn," "Battalion—March," and after having moved them a few paces, " Halt," " Front," " Order Arms," " Stand Easy." An officer who was present states that the effect was most beneficial, the electric shock of the word of command at once rousing the men and giving them something else to think of; they sloped arms and marched as if on the parade-ground, their thoughts, from habit, more concerned with the "three days" they would get if they sloped arms badly, than with the casualties in their ranks caused by the bursting shells.

It is to be noticed that this was the same regiment which fought so well, for ten long hours, in the front line at Gravelotte, which the same Discipline enabled them to achieve.

Prince Kraft zu Hohenlohe-Inglefingen describes a most instructive example of Discipline, which he saw at Sedan, during the attempt of Wimpffen to break out.

"We were standing in position to the east of Givonne, fronting to the west, with the village of Givonne, which was occupied by the Rifles and Fusiliers of the Guard, lying in the deep valley of the Givonne to our front. It was about 1 p.m. The enemy's infantry had drawn back from the opposite edge of the valley of the Givonne,

---

NOTE.—The word " Battalion-March," means in Germany Parade-March, knees kept straight, etc. If " March at Ease" is meant, the word is given, " Ohne Tritt" *i.e.*, without step.

as far as the Bois de la Garenne, which stood on higher ground. A few companies of our infantry had made use of this opportunity to occupy the further edge of the valley. One company of the Rifles of the Guard had done so from Givonne in front of my line of artillery, while in front of the left wing of that line two companies of the "Fran zRegiment" under Captain von C——, advancing from Haybes had taken up a similar position. The last named two companies had crowned the further edge of the valley, and had got under cover in a single thin line of skirmishers. The enemy's artillery fire was as good as silenced.

Suddenly to the south of the Bois de la Garenne a thick mass of the enemy's infantry rushed out of a hollow which extends from the wood to the Fond de Givonne, and charged as hard as they could run on Haybes, and therefore directly on these two companies. I judged the masses of Infantry to amount to 5,000 to 6,000 men.—Though I gave the order as quickly as possible to all the batteries of my line of Artillery, (90 guns) to open a rapid fire on the enemy's masses of infantry, I could not help feeling anxious about the two companies of the "Franz" Regiment, which lay on the other side of the valley of the Givonne."— "Although the shells wrought horrible destruction, the mass still came on nearer and nearer, for the enemy fought with the courage of despair. The moment soon came when I was compelled to order the fire on the head of the column to cease (for fear of hitting the two companies.") "In contrast to the thick smoke which was made by the rapid fire of the French, no fire could be seen to proceed from our two companies. I turned my field-glass on to them, and then at last saw here and there the puff of a discharged rifle; the whole line of skirmishers lay flat on the ground, their rifles at their shoulders and their sights on the target. Captain Von C—, only, walking up and down as gracefully as one often sees him at a ball, moved along his line of skirmishers, and (as he afterwards told me) exhorted them to aim quietly and shoot slowly. But each bullet struck down one of the advancing enemy; the number of those who drew near to the skirmishing line grew less and less; a few even reached the line, and met with their fate at the muzzles of the rifles, for two of our men lie there bayonetted through the back from above. But the whole attack, which was commenced with such boldness, died away. Only a few survivors turned to fly, and were shot down by the pursuing fire of the infantry. The whole mass was destroyed in the space of ten minutes."—The proportion of numbers was 300 to 6,000. "Granted that the 300 were supported by an effective fire of Artillery, and that this destroyed half of the column of attack, yet the odds will still be 3,000 to 300, or ten to one."

Such was the Discipline which rendered the success of "the big battalions" of Germany a certainty; which enabled them, confident in the ability of their troops to fight superior numbers if necessary, to seize every opportunity of striking at the foe, and to hold fast the adversary, often with inferior numbers, till re-inforcements, marching to the cannon-sound, arrived to complete the victory. " Such is the order " was ever a magic word in our army. And even if one half the men fell in carrying it out, yet the other half executed it to the utmost." " It was ordered, therefore, it was done."

It must be remembered that the Discipline of the French which broke up in 1870, which proved itself unable to stand artillery fire, or to retain its cohesion under the storm of breech-loading bullets, was that of a renowned and war-like army, proud of the traditions of a glorious past, and confident in its ability to chain future victory to its eagles. It was composed of brave and warlike soldiers; it was led by gallant officers; it was well practised in Discipline-in-mass, in battalion parades, in showy reviews and marches-past. To what then was the failure of French Discipline due ? The answer seems to be that it was due to the fact that they had not grasped the conditions of modern European battle, consequent on the introduction of the breech-loader. One of the chief facts which, confident in the warlike qualities of their troops, in the gallantry of their leaders, they had not considered, was that Discipline-in-mass was no longer sufficient. They did not understand that, owing to the dissolving effect of the breech-loader and the consequent extended formation of the infantry firing-line, the individual soldier himself had become the ultimate unit of battle, and that Discipline for breech-loading battles must be based upon a thorough individual instruction of each soldier, both in Discipline and in Fire Discipline. So their army fell, and its fall remains as an abiding lesson to all who would not share a similar fate.

CHAPTER V.

DISCIPLINE AS THE FOUNDATION OF FIRE DISCIPLINE.

We have now investigated the subject of Discipline in its relation to the battle-field; we have seen its inestimable, ever-conquering power in the stress of battle; we have also seen of what it consists, namely: the habit of instantaneous, instinctive obedience engrained into the soldier. It is an axiom that, other things being equal or nearly equal, those troops which are better-disciplined, in whom this habit of instinctive obedience is best developed, in whom it has most become an instinct, will ever prove victorious over troops in whom it is not so well-developed.

The only question, therefore, which remains is, how can this habit be developed so as best to suit the conditions of future battle?

In considering this question, we at once come across the great fact that there is a difference between the Discipline which was required before the introduction of breech-loaders and the Discipline which is required since their introduction. The difference is due to what has been called "the dissolving effect" of the breech-loader upon all formations, owing to the depth of the field now swept by effective fire, and to the hail of bullets with which the rapid firing breech-loader enables the beaten zones to be covered.

In the old shoulder to shoulder days it was sufficient if the troops were well-drilled and well-disciplined in the mass, as the influence of such a mass of men moving in order obedient to the word of command, was sufficient to carry forward, and to nullify the counter-influence of such as obeyed the word of command unwillingly. This fact, the following quotation from the "Military Memoirs" of an officer present at Quatre Bras, will exemplify. "In fact, it required no little exertion to keep some of the young soldiers in the ranks, for perceiving the French to be so much more numerous than themselves, and that the garden hedge, though very thick, afforded no protection, the danger appeared to them so very great, that *but for their veteran companions*, and the attention of the officers to their duties, they might have been induced to retire." Therefore, after the recruit had finished his training, battalion drill or training in forming part of a disciplined mass was sufficient to meet the requirements of battle. It is true that the soldier was often required to fight as a skirmisher, but such skirmishing was only a minor operation, and the main thing was the fighting in a close-order disciplined mass. Therefore, battalion drill or Discipline-in-mass was practically sufficient.

Since the introduction of the long ranging, rapid firing breech-loader, however, such battalion Discipline-in-mass has become no longer sufficient. We have now to suit our Discipline to the fact that all close-order formations must change into extended-order formations when they come under effective fire. We have also to suit it to the further fact, that these extended-order formations will resolve themselves frequently into the pell-mell mixed firing line of a breech-loading battle; that is to say, on many parts of the battle-field, especially opposite those important points of the hostile position selected for assault, where it is necessary to bring up the firing line to its utmost possible strength, where reinforcements can only be brought up in rear, and where it will often be necessary to pile battalion on battalion, that opposite such points the firing line must become a mixture of units, that opposite such points the soldier will frequently find himself separated from his accustomed leaders, and forced, during the utmost din and confusion of battle, to form himself into part of a new unit (possibly with strangers of other regiments) under a new (and possibly completely strange) leader.

This decisive pell-mell firing line of breech loader battle can only be reduced to order by the strictest Fire Discipline. *The first condition, therefore, of a modern Discipline suited to the necessities of a modern battle, is that, it be regarded as the foundation, and be governed by the requirements of Fire Discipline.*

The dominating importance of Fire Discipline was strongly brought out during the war in Chili, 1891, where the new magazine small-bore rifles were first used. The badly-disciplined troops of Balmaceda completely broke up before the rapidity and accuracy of the Mannlicher rifle, which, in a few minutes, destroyed all cohesion amongst the troops; the advance consequently came to a stand-still at distances of 1,000 and 1,600 metres. On the other hand, among the Congress troops, the great difficulty was the enormous expenditure of ammunition. Each soldier had 180 cartridges, but some detachments fired it all away in from half to three-quarters of an hour, and on the 21st August, the Infantry, as a whole, at the close of the battle, had only six rounds left, and it was impossible to replenish their ammunition till next morning; that is to say, they would have been helpless against another attack. The troops on both sides were, of course, badly-disciplined and insufficiently trained, but we must not on that account neglect the lessons to be derived from their conduct. If the rapidity and accuracy of the Mannlicher rifle was sufficient to destroy, in a few minutes, all cohesion among badly-disciplined troops and to stop their advance at distances of 1,000 and 1,600 metres, it is manifest that only by the very strictest Discipline can even trained soldiers be led forward under its fire, and that only by an iron Fire

Discipline thoroughly engrained into every soldier's blood, only by constant practice in the "pell-mell" mixed firing line can we hope to bring the close fire fight to a successful conclusion. If undisciplined troops fired away 180 cartridges in from half to three-quarters of an hour, it is manifest that the same result will follow with trained troops if once the "control" of the fire be lost, unless the soldier has previously been thoroughly trained in "fighting on by himself." It all points to the absolutely dominating importance of Fire Discipline, and to the fact that the Discipline of the future (or, rather, of to-day, for the right course cannot be too soon adopted), must anxiously seek out and base itself upon the requirements of Fire Discipline.

The Discipline of the present must therefore regard in agreement with Fire Discipline, the individual soldier as the ultimate unit of battle, and base its system of training on a thorough individual instruction of each soldier ; otherwise, it cannot meet the requirements of Fire Discipline, and properly prepare the soldier for modern battle conditions.

Such being the case, the question still remains, how can this necessary individual training of the soldier be best met by our system of battalion instruction ?

No great difficulty is here apparent. It is merely requisite that a slight change in the system of instruction be introduced; that the company shall be made the unit of instruction in future, instead of the battalion ;

and that the company commander shall be the instructor, instead of the Adjutant and Sergeant-Major.

The first essential condition of decentralization of battalion organization is that the Adjutant should be relieved of his executive functions, and his position be assimilated to that of an Adjutant of Artillery. Under this arrangement he would become a staff officer pure and simple, his duties would be confined to those of administration, and his executive work would devolve upon the company commanders.

The system of instruction-in-mass, of constant battalion parades, can no longer meet the battle-requirements of to-day, for it cannot meet the first demand of Fire Discipline, namely that the individual soldier be regarded as the ultimate unit of battle, and that his whole training, therefore, be based upon a system of thorough individual instruction.

The system of battalion instruction-in-mass is unable to meet this requirement of modern battle, because the number of men on parade is manifestly too large to enable the necessary attention to be given to each individual. Also, owing to the system of instruction-in-mass, the company commanders can so seldom get their men apart from battalion parades, that they are unable to give them that individual attention which they could otherwise do. The period of company military training is so short, and so many things have to be taught in that limited time, that it affords no opportunity for thorough individual instruction.

If, therefore, the system of instruction-in-mass can no longer meet the battle requirements of the present, it is manifest that it must give place to a system which can do so; to a system of company individual instruction under the company commander as instructor.

The system of company instruction under the company commander has already been partly introduced, during the periods of company military training and musketry. It now only remains that the instruction of the soldier in Discipline and in Fire Discipline be likewise placed in the hands of his company commander, in the hands of that leader whom he must follow in battle.

This seems so simple and natural a step, that it is difficult at first to realize all the benefits which will follow. It is difficult at first to realize that this simple step is all that is required to mark the transition from the Discipline of the past to the Discipline of the present; from the system of instruction-in-mass to the system of individual instruction. Yet such is the case. If only this step be conceded, then the thorough, individual instruction of every single soldier, without exception will be possible, and will soon be the rule, in every company.

The company commander is acquainted with each individual soldier and his capabilities, and with how much extra attention should be bestowed upon each dull or awkward individual. He will, therefore, be able to carry out the thorough, individual instruction of every single soldier in his company, in Discipline and in Fire

Discipline; in the habit of instinctive obedience acquired through exact, instantaneous smartness in the muscular movements of marching, turning, and handling of arms; also in the habit of instinctively falling into new units out of a pell-mell of old units, and in the habit of correctly "fighting on by himself," when without leaders. Under his constant supervision, his section and sub-section leaders can train every single individual to the requisite degree of smartness in these few requirements, practising the dull or awkward individually again and again, till a uniform habit of exact, instantaneous, instinctive obedience to the word of command has been acquired by the whole company. By such means the company will become a thoroughly handy unit, each individual soldier thoroughly trained, in Discipline and in Fire Discipline, under that leader whom he will follow on the battle-fields of the coming war.

If anyone should doubt the perfect ability of company leaders thus to train their men in Discipline and in Fire Discipline, let him go to Germany, and there watch the exercises of companies trained on this system; let him there watch these companies being exercised as units of a Battalion, in perfect close-order drill :— and he will doubt no longer, for he will have seen what the system of individual instruction can do.

In our own Army, we see that the system of decentralization of command and training has been carried out in the Artillery with complete success. The battery system is so organized as to give every officer distinct and definite duties in the training of the battery for its work in the field. There is a practical chain of responsibility extending from the battery commander downwards through all ranks to the individual gunner. The regimental regulations of the Royal Artillery direct that the battery commander should work in all things through his section officers. The battery is divided into three sections, each commanded by a subaltern; that command is a real one, not a nominal one. He conducts, and is solely responsible for, the efficient training of his section on the lines laid down by the battery commander, and for its discipline and interior economy. Artillery adjutants have no executive functions; the system of each officer entirely training his own men produces the very best results, and has been officially ordered.

There is another most important point in connection with the system of company instruction under the company commanders, which must not be lost sight of. It is this:—that this is the system which tends best to develop in company officers those habits of command, self-reliance, judgment, and initiative, which the necessary delegation of command on a modern battle-field renders imperative. The necessity for this delegation of command is insisted on constantly in our new Infantry Drill, 1893. For instance, it is stated (Section 114-6) "Responsibility also which formerly rested with superior officers, must now be delegated to subordinates. To use, and not to abuse, this, demands habits of self-reliance, coupled with a strict sense of duty and Discipline. *Unless these habits are inculcated during peace, it cannot be expected that they will suddenly be developed during war,"* &c.

Such being the case, how can an officer be so well trained to accept responsibility in war, as by having been accustomed to it during peace ? What better preparation can there be for leading a company with judgment and discretion in war, than by having constantly and thoroughly trained it, and led it over all ground and under all circumstances, in peace ? What can give a company commander that thorough knowledge of the capabilities of his men, which is so useful and necessary in war, so well as having trained them all individually himself ? Will not an officer take more pride and interest in his men during peace, and more care of them in war, when he knows and has individually trained every man amongst them ? Will not the men, too, have a more thorough trust and confidence in their company officers, and follow them more staunchly and cheerfully in war, when each individual has learnt from them all he knows, and has been accustomed to look to them alone for everything in peace ? The advantages of the system of company individual instruction are, however, so numerous and apparent, that it is unnecessary to accumulate further instances, for they are well known to all.

If it be granted that the system of Discipline must

accommodate itself to the battle conditions of to-day, that the Discipline of the present must bare itself upon the dominating requirements of Fire Discipline, then the system of company individual instruction by the company commanders follows as a natural corollary. Only by this system can the first great requirement of Fire Discipline be met, the requirement that the individual soldier be regarded as the ultimate unit of battle, and that, therefore, every single soldier, without exception, be thoroughly trained in Discipline, in instinctive obedience.

This result can be at once achieved if the company be recognised as the unit of instruction in all things. Three or four days a week can be set apart for company training under the company commanders, on the basis of a thorough individual instruction of every soldier. One or two days a week can be set apart for working the combined units together, in close-order drill or in tactical exercises, and for instructing the company officers. During the days set apart for company training, the company commanders can practise their men in whatever they find most necessary, in close-order drill and handling of arms, in Fire Discipline, or in field exercises. On these days, the company officers and non-commissioned officers, under supervision of the company commander, can give the necessary individual instruction to each single soldier, in whatever part of his duty in Discipline, or in Fire Discipline, the company commander may order. It will not matter if the company parades are often small, for the object being *individual instruction*, this can be attained equally well even if only a few men are present; valuable instruction in marching, in turning, in handling of arms, in Fire Discipline, in musketry, in outposts, in patrolling, in the use of the bayonet, can be given even to the smallest number of men who will ever turn out on a company parade.

Such a system of company instruction, to which three or four days each week are devoted, will render it unnecessary that a special period be set apart for company military training, for it will be going on all the year round. Instead thereof, a period of a month or six weeks could be set apart for battalion field exercises in the autumn, when the crops are off the ground. During this period the companies could be practised together in carrying out any series of tactical exercises which the battalion commander may determine upon, so as best to complete their warlike instruction, and best to train the company officers in executing any tactical task, with that mutual co-operation, judgment, and discretion, rendered imperative by their new responsibilities.

An unprejudiced open-minded consideration of the battle conditions of to-day, a consideration undertaken, not with the view of finding arguments to support any particular opinion, but with the view of arriving at the truth, must, surely, convince every soldier that the system of instruction-in-mass, though once sufficient, is now no longer sufficient to meet the requirements of battle. It will, surely, convince him that our modern Discipline must now base itself upon the requirements of Fire Discipline, upon the individual training of every single soldier. It will also, surely, convince him that the only method by which this condition of individual instruction can be properly met, is by the system of company individual instruction under the company commanders. If this be true, then, bearing in mind the fact that those troops whose Discipline was best suited to the battle conditions of the day, have ever proved victorious in war, surely it were wisest for us to at once adopt the system of a thorough individual instruction both in Discipline and in Fire Discipline.

It is impossible to tell how soon we may find ourselves arrayed in battle against European troops armed with shrapnel and magazine rifles, so it behoves us to look to our Discipline. If it be true that the system of individual instruction in Discipline and in Fire Discipline, can alone meet the requirements of modern battle, it must be wisest to adopt it at once, now, while there is yet time, before the coming war is upon us.

CHAPTER VI.

SUMMARY.

The reason, the necessity, and the requirements of strict Discipline must now stand out clear to the intelligence of every non-commissioned officer and private soldier. We see that, all through history, victory has attended those troops who were better disciplined than their adversaries. We see that this Discipline can only come as the result of a long course of patient training in peace ; that its distinguishing characteristic is exact, instantaneous obedience; that the manner in which this habit of exact obedience is taught varies according to the arms and tactics of the period, and the conditions of battle in which it is meant to be applied. We see that modern Discipline recognises the fact of the dissolving effect of the long-ranging, rapid-firing breech-loader upon all formations, and is therefore based upon the axiom that *the individual soldier is the ultimate unit of battle.* It is therefore required that every individual soldier, every ultimate unit of battle, shall be thoroughly disciplined. It is required that every single individual soldier, who may form part of a future pell-mell firing line, shall be thoroughly imbued with the habit of exact instinctive, muscular obedience to the word of command, so that, in the utmost stress of modern battle, under the heaviest hail of magazine rifle bullets, even if his mind be too astounded to attend, yet his muscles shall instinctively obey. This habit of instinctive obedience is required, because, under such circumstances, the soldier is often too confused to act except on instinct; his instinct of obedience, therefore, must be stronger than his instinct of self-preservation, or than his instinct to fire wildly at the enemy. If he is not capable of such obedience, if he is not properly disciplined, then nothing can be expected on a European battle-field but confusion, disaster, and death. Therefore the strictest Discipline, that which most insists on the habit of instinctive obedience being properly cultivated in peace, *is the kindest to the soldier, has his interest more at heart, and will prove his greatest aid in battle.* The soldier has no greater enemies, no more insidious foes, no more treacherous friends than those who clamour for a relaxation of Discipline.

This fact the following passage from the account given by Major Henderson of the struggle for the Gifert-Wald, ("The Battle of Spicheren," 5-6 p.m.,) where is described the conquering power of the stricter German Discipline, as opposed to the weaker Discipline of the French, will illustrate. "But the Prussian infantry was true to its Discipline and training; and, when, in the turmoil and excitement of the fight, the soldiers found that they were parted from their immediate commander, or that their own leader had fallen, they sought out the nearest officer, irrespective of the number on his shoulder-straps, and looked to him for orders."—" *Nor, although on both sides there was equality in courage and in numbers, was there much doubt as to the result.* Here, swarming up from the hollow and across the leafy ridge, with their faces set towards Spicheren, *were men with deep instincts of obedience, trusting their leaders and following the slightest sign*; here were officers trained in battle exercises, seeing, in the deadly strife which raged in the thickets, but a livelier picture of their accustomed work, and recalling without effort the shifts and expedients learnt in more peaceful autumns ; gathering as it were by mere force of habit, the scattered files together ; cheering and directing, thrusting ceaselessly at the flank of hostile groups, recognising clearly the purpose of the fight, and accepting as readily, as composedly, the responsibilities that the situation forced upon them. Opposed to them were men *staunch and impetuous, but ill-disciplined*; each fighting for his own hand, and relying more on the rapidity than the accuracy of their fire; *vigorous in individual effort, but regardless of their leaders,* and ignorant of the power of united action."—" And so, by six o'clock, superior training, skill, and Discipline,

---

NOTE.—The italics here are added by the writer.

prevailed against mere courage,—the wood was yielded, and the Prussians lined the southern border." We here see vividly portrayed the victorious power in battle of a strict Discipline during peace. We further see, on the other hand, the state to which even the proudest and showiest troops may be brought in European battle, when their masses are broken up, if their training during peace has not been such as to insist on the habit of exact instinctive obedience on the part of every single soldier. Every non-commissioned officer and private soldier should bear this contrast always in mind, and remember that the object of the regulations and restraints of Discipline, of the exact, instantaneous obedience demanded,—is that he may be able to fight victoriously in such a struggle, with the power of strict Discipline.

Every private soldier who permits himself to slowly or partially obey a command, every non-commissioned officer who passes over any instance of such slow or partial obedience, is individually weakening the habit of instinctive obedience, and unknowingly preparing for himself the fate of the confused and ill-disciplined on a European battle-field. Every private soldier who permits himself to offend against subordination, every non-commissioned officer who overlooks any such offence, is striking at the root of Discipline, undoing the beneficial effect of previous training, and tending to prepare for himself and comrades, disaster in the coming war.

It is not, however, sufficient to merely recognise in theory the power of strict Discipline. Probably, the French in 1870 perfectly understood its importance theoretically—only they did not carry theory into practice. It is necessary for us, in view of the coming war, not only to recognise in theory the importance of the habit of instinctive obedience, but to cultivate and carry it out now during peace. How this habit of instinctive obedience can be acquired now, during peace, we have already seen. We have seen that the foundation is that every word of command must be obeyed exactly and instantaneously, without the slightest slowness or intervening working of the mind; that this instantaneous obedience must be practised till the muscles obey the word of command almost independently of the mind, almost involuntarily. The muscles, as we have seen, which can be thus trained, are those of the legs, feet, and arms, hence the importance of the utmost possible smartness in the motions of marching at "Attention," of turning, and of handling the rifle. We see that the smartness of the motions is the test of the degree to which the muscles have been trained in this habit of instinctive obedience, and that slow, careless motions indicate a limited power of obedience, and a badly-disciplined mind. We have further seen that in these motions, the indications of exact and instinctive obedience, it is necessary for purposes of Fire Discipline that every single individual soldier, however dull or awkward, must be practised again and again till he has attained the same level of excellence as the rest of his comrades; because, in the pell-mell of battle, there must be no men there who are not trained to instinctive obedience.

It is further apparent that it must never be permitted that this habit of instinctive obedience learnt on the parade ground, be interfered with by any habit of slow or partial obedience acquired off the parade ground. For this reason, whenever the soldier is called to "Attention" off the parade ground, the same smartness in all his motions must be insisted on as if he were marching past. For the same reason, also, exact and unquestioning obedience must be exacted to any order in quarters, and no instance of disrespect or insubordination to superiors in rank must ever be overlooked.

It must now be clear to every intelligent soldier that *the strictest Discipline is the kindest in the long run*. It must be clear that an idea which has lately found expression, an idea which may be called "the voluntary-soldier-to-be-treated-kindly" idea, is no kindness to him, if it be interpreted as meaning a relaxation of Discipline, but, on the contrary, is injurious; for any relaxation of Discipline can only lead him to confusion, disaster, and death, in the coming war, while strict Discipline will carry him victoriously through the coming struggle strong in its conquering power.

When the soldier finds himself thoroughly engrained

with this spirit of instinctive obedience, when he has come to look upon an "order" as sacred, when he has come to take a pride in belonging to a body of men of whom this spirit, combined with Loyalty and Patriotism, is the distinguishing characteristic, when he has come to take a pride in performing every military motion with the utmost possible smartness ; then—and not till then—can he call himself, in the true meaning of the term, a soldier. When he has learnt to take this pride in the possession of a characteristic which none but a soldier can possess, as it can only be acquired by his long course of training, then he will understand what is meant by "*the pride of arms,*" by the feeling that, as a soldier, he stands above all civilians, above all who do not serve their country. He will then begin to take a proper pride in himself as a soldier, and in the exact and smart performance of all those observances of military etiquette, which are the outward expression of this feeling. He will then endeavour to distinguish himself as much as possible from civilians, having regard to the honour of the uniform, by his superior bearing and behaviour. In the words of Sir Charles Napier : " Soldiers should be, in thought and reality, identified with their country's glory—the proudest of her sons."

www.ingramcontent.com/pod-product-compliance
Lightning Source LLC
Chambersburg PA
CBHW060219050426
42446CB00013B/3110